Chapter 1: Introduction

I am a medical doctor born in Burundi, my beloved and great nation located in Africa specifically in East Africa.

After my birth at hospital, my dearest father was asked what name he wanted me to be called. He said:"Nizigiyimana" meaning" In God we trust ".

In other words, I was cast on God the creator of Heaven and the earth since my birthday. Hope you understand why I love the great people of America because of their "In God we trust" slogan.

Burundi has an ethnical issue - like hatred between my beloved

great people Hutu and my beloved
great people Tutsi- that had
been pulling down the country
for many years instead of going
forward.

I thank God I have been
protected from being under
influence of stereotypes against
my different ethnical people.

The great Burundi has three (3)
different types of people
called:" Hutu, Tutsi and Twa."
They are all great. I love my
father and mother because they
never talked to me about Hutu
people as my enemies. His
friends are Hutu and Tutsi. I
grew up in that atmosphere of
loving all people including the
great people who used to be
neglected in Burundi, my beloved
and great people of Twa. Whether
minority or majority we are all

one people that must live together as one great nation one Burundi.

At university there were two (2) blocks of Hutu and Tutsi. Tutsi students would find themselves almost alone without Hutu and so Hutu students would find themselves almost alone without Tutsi among them.

You know what? I would go among the Hutu students and make them my friend and they were always asking me:" Who are you? I am a child of God. Maybe when they looked at me they could see me looking like Tutsi but they were confused because I was always with them some time and some time with Tutsi students. I am proud of that behavior.

A human being is a human being! I have to love everybody! Why

hating a human being like you?
Why not desiring to see other
people doing well like you? When
you practice love you are
promoting yourself!

I used to say to myself I am
Hutu, I am Tutsi, I am TWA. All
of them are my beloved people
and I am proud of that. I stayed
in a house with Hutu people my
people. One of them I used to
call her as my "mother." That
great woman of God but late now
used to take care of me like her
beloved son. She was a woman who
loved to help people. Her
husband -who used to beat her
because she was not giving birth
to male children- before he
passed away, used to call her
"UNHCR United Nations High
Commissioner for
Refugees." because she was
helping everyone. And the more

she helps other people the more
God continued to make her
richer. I thank God for having
given her later a son, who came
as a "savior" to her against the
unfounded hate of her husband.

One day that mother wanted to
pay for me the school fees at a
private university but I did not
get a place and continued at the
public University called "the
University of Burundi." She was
ready for anything that can make
me happy. Her children are like
my sisters and my brother. You
see how blessed I was? God can
use a very person for your
goodness that is why it is not
good to despise other people.
You do not know who has been
ordained to take you to your
destination. That is a secret of
God unless it is revealed unto
you. There is a reason why you

are with someone together for the first time or many times, be grateful for that and talk to each other nicely.

Therefore, stop limiting yourself and lock up to yourself in your small tribe, race, nation... Start seeing yourself as a world citizen. No matter how rich your nation maybe it is not a reason to cut relationship with so called poor nations as long as they are human beings like you. They have hands you may need ; therefore look how you can help them to get developed like you because you will find that you are making yourself more developed and more richer.

Today in Zambia the people that are strengthening me or blessing me are not Burundians or members

of my family but they are people
of this wonderful nation of
Zambia. Be thankful to God for
who you are and be grateful to
God also for your brothers and
sisters who are black or white
because God created people with
different skin colors for your
own good and happiness. Love
everyone!

My prayer is to see *One Rwanda
one People"* and one *Burundi one
Nation* like what my beloved and
great people of Zambia a great
nation with more than 73
tribes did as *"One Zambia one
Nation."*

Imagine if we form one nation
great nation where all nations
from all over the world are
found themselves and use
English as an official
language just to unite all the

nations under one King and always before the news we hear "One world one nation" like in my great beloved people of Zambia. Imagine if we are united as one powerful nation through ties of love to each other and make great our great world nation! Only in this way we are going to overcome poverty and wars between nations because there will be no more of "this is my territory, this is our water". There will be no need of nuclear weapon that my beloved and great people of Iran and North Korea are trying by all means to possess like other powerful nations.

My beloved and great people of China, Russia and United States of America will be working together as one people with the entire whole world developing

all together including my
beloved and great people of
Africa. Those trillions of US
dollars we are spending in
military will be spent against
poverty. There will be no space
war at all because the space
belongs to all of us. Why fight
for the things we did not
create?

Zambia is not ashamed in their
tribes. It is an easy thing to
ask a tribe of a Zambian which
is not easy in Burundi or
Rwanda. When I see people who
resemble Tutsi or Hutu in
Burundi or Rwanda in Zambian
people and they do not hate each
other because their noise like
in Burundi or Rwanda.

If in Zambia they cannot hate
and kill each other because of
their noise why not stop that

stupidity of killing each other
for generations in Burundi and
Rwanda forever and build a
strong nation without any hatred
based on the appearance of
somebody's noise. Enough is
enough!

Forget the killing in the past
and come together and form one
strong new Burundi one people
and one strong new Rwanda, one
people. *Choose forgiveness and
love one another.*

I do not like to be in one box.
Every human being is my friend
my brother, my sister. Black,
White, Chinese, people Asiatic…
as long as they are human beings
I love them and they are my
people. They can feel hungry
like me, they can be happy like
me therefore we as human beings

are one and must live together
as one and help each other as
one world great nation without
borders. A world without egoism.
A world that shares technology
easily with other nations
because we are all human beings
condemned to better our lives
with dignity.

At university, one of my friends
was a Hutu and very intelligent,
Hutu people have been into power
for many years in Burundi.

If you want to overcome some of
stereotypes you have accepted
effortlessly because of what you
heard against other people from
your different leaders or
ancestors, it is easy and you
will always find that what you
were told is a fake information
and that there is no reason of
hating each other.

I remember when I took oath as a medical doctor in Burundi, I held the Burundian flag by faith as a "world flag". All nations are my people. I am a medical doctor for all nations and I am proud of that.

I like to watch news not of the local news but also international news. Why? I want to know what is happening around the globe. I am concerned of what happening around the globe and think what can be done as solution to different issues. Today God has made our world too small to live without knowing what happening around the globe almost instantly. We are in the right time of gathering all nations of our beautiful world into one great nation.

A friend of mine asked me one day why I like to watch those international news through these great main media like CNN, FOX news, France 24; Aljazeera... where they show almost only the bad news. "I want to know what is happening around the world with my people from all over the world so that I can pray for them." I replied to her. I believe prayer is powerful because God does perform miracles through prayers!

"Why have you come to work at our clinic? Is it not to wait for the patients who are coming with their health issues and give a solution for them to come out of their bad conditions?" I asked her again. She kept quiet like someone convinced.

People should not fear to watch news nationally and internationally for them to be a solution to the different people of our beloved and great world. You can pray for any problem that is emerging in any part of the world and bring a change. And the Father in heaven who sees in secret will reward you! The time will never allow you to be isolationist! What is hitting in South Arabia is also hitting the global economy. As the whole world, we form one body, it Hurricane is hitting America it is also hitting the whole body: The whole world!

When I was first called David?

When I was 11 years old, I was given a new name in my local Pentecostal church in an area called Kibenga right in the

Capital city of Bujumbura.
What's that?"David" was the new
name given to me. Jesus says "I
tell you the truth, whatever you
forbid on earth will be
forbidden in heaven, and
whatever you permit on earth
will be permitted in
heaven." Matthew 18:18, New
Living Translation.

So that name given in my great
church was also permitted in
heaven.

A certain Sunday that I will
never forget I asked one of the
leaders to give a time to
testify how I got born again. As
small as I was, the pulpit was
taller than me then they had to
put me on the drum for me to be
able to speak facing the
audience holding the microphone
in my hands. At the end of my

testimony, a man of God who was leading said:" You are David".

The church started calling me "David". In other words, the man of God said you are like David the one who fought against Goliath in the name of the Lord Yahweh and won using a stone and a slinger without a sword in his hands.

David cut off his head and later on became a king after the heart of God over the Israel who was the people of God in all the Earth before Jesus died for all nations for all generations. Hope you understand why I love the people of Israel as my own people and Arabs people because they share one ancestor "Abraham".

These great people they are brothers. They must love each

other between themselves and between them and all Christians because all the people became children of Abraham through our dearest Jesus the MESSIAH! Whether you believe it or not you cannot change it. A car is a car whether you believe it or not!

While at University in the medical faculty, I put on that name of "DAVID" cheerfully and wholeheartedly. I received the spirit of David I said to my God who is the Father of the Whole World:'' *Heavenly Father may you use me seven times the same way you used King David in his time in the name of Jesus Christ but protect me from the weakness of King David and those of King Solomon. I want to make a difference! Both King David and King Solomon did something that*

*gave occasion to the enemies of
the LORD to blaspheme. I even
told the Lord to make me wiser
and wealthier than king Solomon
and keep me from doing wrong
against his laws. I want to
shame the devil. In short, I
want to please my Lord Jesus
Christ by making a difference. I
want to be a rich king through
holy ways and still love God and
His people as a husband of one
wife. I want badly to change
what King Solomon did. I do not
know why but that it is a burden
in me!*

   *I give myself to you Lord
Jesus to rule like your king
David over all nations because
you died for all nations without
exception of any nation around
the globe in your name of Jesus
Christ!"*

I started reading the bible to know who David whose name means "beloved" was.

As, I was reading the bible I found out that the same way I was cast to the Lord and pushed to trust in God through my surname from my mother's breast, King David also was pushed to trust in the Lord since his mother's breast: "*Yet you brought me out of the womb; you made me trust in you, even at my mother's breast.*
From birth I was cast on you;
    from my mother's womb you have been my
God."Psalm22:10, New International Version (NIV).

Why this resemblance? I always ask myself. Simple coincidence? I know that nothing happen by accident.

Another resemblance with King David: When my mother was still alive, she is the one who used to share the word of God at home. She would organize how to pray. She was committed in serving the Lord. She used to sing in a choir and she liked that so much. I used to escort her when she was going to visit different people at their place and share the Word of God with them. She was my really my friend and I loved her a lot.

The way I was too closed to my mother was the same connection that King David had with his mother. How I know that?

That is very simple question because King David said:"*Truly I am your servant, LORD; I serve you just as my mother did; you have freed me from my*

chains.” Psalm 116Psalm116:16,
New International Version.

That means that King David was
most connected to his mother
than to his father. The bible
does not tell us about the
mother of David. Why David was
the person behind the sheep of
his father? Why the father
forgot about him when the
prophet of the Yahweh came to
anoint one of his sons to become
king of Israel to unseat King
Saul?

I used to wonder why until I
read the following article about
the mother of King David by this
great woman Chana Weisber

Nitzevet, Mother of David

The bold voice of silence

*Save me, O God, for the waters
threaten to engulf me. . .*

*I am wearied by my calling out,
and my throat is dry. I've lost
hope in waiting. . .*

*More numerous than the hairs on
my head are those who hate me
without reason. . .*

*Must I then repay what I have
not stolen?*

*Mighty are those who would cut
me down, who are my enemies
without cause. . .*

*O God, You know my folly, and my
unintended wrongs are not hidden
from you. . .*

*It is for your sake that I have
borne disgrace, that humiliation
covers my face.*

*I have become a stranger to my
brothers, an alien to my
mother's sons.*

*Out of envy for Your House, they
ravaged me; the disgraces of
those who revile you have fallen
upon me. . .*

*Those who sit by the gate talk
about me. I am the taunt of
drunkards. . .*

*Disgrace breaks my heart, and I
am left deathly sick.*

*I hope for solace, but there is
none; and for someone to comfort
me, but I find no one.*

*They put gall into my meal, and
give me vinegar to quench my
thirst. . .* (Psalm 69)[1]

This psalm describes the life of a poor, despised and lowly individual, who lacks even a single friend to comfort him. It is the voice of a tormented soul who has experienced untold humiliation and disgrace. Through no apparent cause of his own, he is surrounded by enemies who wish to cut him down; even his own brothers are strangers to him, ravaging and reviling him.

Amazingly, this is the voice of the mighty King David, righteous and beloved servant of God, feared and awed by all.

King David had many challenges throughout his life. But at what point did this great individual feel so alone, so disgraced, and so undeserving of love and friendship?

What caused King David to face such an intense ignominy, to be shunned by his own brothers in his home ("I have become a stranger to my brothers"), by the Torah sages who sat in judgment at the gates ("those who sit by the gate talk about me") and by the drunkards on the street corners ("I am the taunt of drunkards")? What had King David done to arouse such ire and contempt? And was there no one, at this time in his life, which would provide him with love, comfort and friendship?

This psalm, in which King David passionately gives voice to the heaviest burdens of his soul, refers to a period of twenty-eight years, from his earliest childhood until he was coroneted as king of the people
of Israel by the prophet Samuel.

David was born into the illustrious family of Yishai (Jesse), who served as the head of the *Sanhedrin* (supreme court of Torah law), and was one of the most distinguished leaders of his generation. Yishai was a man of such greatness that the Talmud (Shabbat 55b) observes that "Yishai was one of only four righteous individuals who died solely due to the instigation of the serpent"—i.e., only because death was decreed upon the human race when Adam and Eve ate from the Tree of Knowledge at the serpent's instigation, not due to any sin or flaw of his own. David was the youngest in his family, which included seven other illustrious and charismatic brothers.

Yet, when David was born, this prominent family greeted his birth with utter derision and contempt. As David describes quite literally in the psalm, "I was a stranger to my brothers, a foreigner to my mother's sons. . . they put gall in my meal, and gave me vinegar to quench my thirst."

David was not permitted to eat with the rest of his family, but was assigned to a separate table in the corner. He was given the task of shepherd because "they hoped that a wild beast would come and kill him while he was performing his duties,"[2] and for this reason was sent to pasture in dangerous areas full of lions and bears.[3]

Only one individual throughout David's youth was pained by his

unjustified plight, and felt a
deep and unconditional bond of
love for the child whom she
alone knew was undoubtedly pure.

This was King David's
mother, Nitzevet bat Adael, who
felt the intensity of her
youngest child's pain and
rejection as her own.

Torn and anguished by David's
unwarranted degradation, yet
powerless to stop it, Nitzevet
stood by the sidelines, in
solidarity with him, shunned
herself, as she too cried rivers
of tears, awaiting the time when
justice would be served. It
would take twenty-eight long
years of assault and rejection,
suffering and degradation until
that justice would finally begin
to materialize.

David's Birth

Why was the young David so reviled by his brothers and people?

To understand the hatred directed toward David, we need to investigate the inner workings behind the events, the secret episodes that aren't recorded in the prophetic books but are alluded to in Midrashim.[4]

David's father, Yishai, was the grandson of Boaz and Ruth. After several years of marriage to his wife, Nitzevet, and after having raised several virtuous children, Yishai began to entertain personal doubts about his ancestry. True, he was the leading Torah authority of his day, but his grandmother Ruth was a convert from the nation of Moab, as related in the book of Ruth.

During Ruth's lifetime, many individuals were doubtful about the legitimacy of her marriage to Boaz. The Torah specifically forbids an Israelite to marry a Moabite convert, since this is the nation that cruelly refused the Jewish people passage through their land, or food and drink to purchase, when they wandered in the desert after being freed from Egypt.

Boaz and the sages understood this law—as per the classic interpretation transmitted in the "Oral Torah"—as forbidding intermarriage with converted *male* Moabites (who were the ones responsible for the cruel conduct), while exempting female Moabite converts. With his marriage to Ruth, Boaz hoped to clarify and publicize this Torah law, which was still unknown to the masses.

Boaz died the night after his marriage with Ruth. Ruth had conceived and subsequently gave birth to their son Oved, the father of Yishai. Some rabble-rousers at the time claimed that Boaz's death verified that his marriage to Ruth the Moabite had indeed been forbidden.

Time would prove differently. Once Oved (so called because he was a true *oved*, servant of God), and later Yishai and his offspring, were born, their righteous conduct and prestigious positions proved the legitimacy of their ancestry. It was impossible that men of such caliber could have descended from a forbidden union.

However, later in his life,
doubt gripped at Yishai's heart,
gnawing away at the very
foundation of his existence.
Being the sincere individual
that he was, his integrity
compelled him to action.

If Yishai's status was
questionable, he was not
permitted to remain married to
his wife, a veritable Israelite.
Disregarding the personal
sacrifice, Yishai decided the
only solution would be to
separate from her, no longer
engaging in marital relations.
Yishai's children were aware of
this separation.

After a number of years had
passed, Yishai longed for a
child whose ancestry would be
unquestionable. His plan was to

engage in relations with his Canaanite maidservant.

He said to her: "I will be freeing you conditionally. If my status as a Jew is legitimate, then you are freed as a proper Jewish convert to marry me. If, however, my status is blemished and I have the legal status of a Moabite convert forbidden to marry an Israelite, I am not giving you your freedom; but as a *shifchah k'naanit*, a Canaanite maidservant, you may marry a Moabite convert."

The maidservant was aware of the anguish of her mistress, Nitzevet. She understood her pain in being separated from her husband for so many years. She knew, as well, of Nitzevet's longing for more children.

The empathetic maidservant secretly approached Nitzevet and informed her of Yishai's plan, suggesting a bold counter plan.

"Let us learn from your ancestress and replicate their actions. Switch places with me tonight, just as Leah did with Rachel," she advised.

With a prayer on her lips that her plan succeeds, Nitzevet took the place of her maidservant. That night, Nitzevet conceived. Yishai remained unaware of the switch.

After three months, Nitzevet's pregnancy became obvious. Incensed, her sons wished to kill their apparently adulterous mother and the "illegitimate" fetus that she carried. Nitzevet, for her part, would not embarrass her husband by revealing the truth of what had occurred. Like her ancestress Tamar, who was prepared to be burned alive rather than embarrass Judah,[5] Nitzevet chose a vow of silence. And like Tamar, Nitzevet would be rewarded for her silence with a child of greatness who would be the forebear of <u>Moshiach</u>.

Unaware of the truth behind his wife's pregnancy, but having compassion on her, Yishai ordered his sons not to touch her. "Do not kill her! Instead, let the child that will be born be treated as a lowly and despised servant. In this way everyone will realize that his status is questionable and, as an illegitimate child, he will not marry an Israelite."

From the time of his birth
onwards, then, Nitzevet's son
was treated by his brothers as
an abominable outcast.[6] Noting
the conduct of his brothers, the
rest of the community assumed
that this youth was a
treacherous sinner full of
unspeakable guilt.

On the infrequent occasions that
Nitzevet's son would return from
the pastures to his home
in Beit Lechem (Bethlehem), he
was shunned by the townspeople.
If something was lost or stolen,
he was accused as the natural
culprit, and ordered, in the
words of the psalm, to "repay
what I have not stolen."

Eventually, the entire lineage
of Yishai was questioned, as
well as the basis of the
original law of the Moabite

convert. People claimed that all
the positive qualities of Boaz
became manifest in Yishai and
his illustrious seven sons,
while all the negative character
traits from Ruth the Moabite
clung to this despicable
youngest son.

Anointing King David

We are first introduced to David
when the prophet Samuel is
commanded to go to Beit Lechem
to anoint a new king, to replace
the rejected King Saul.

Samuel arrives in Beit Lechem,
and the elders of the city come
out to greet him, nervous at
this unusual and unexpected
visit, since the elderly prophet
had stopped circulating
throughout the land. The elders
feared that Samuel had heard
about a grievous sin that was

taking place in their
city.[7] Perhaps he had come to
rebuke them over the behavior of
Yishai's despised shepherd boy,
living in their midst.

Samuel declared, however, that
he had come in peace, and asked
the elders, and Yishai and his
sons, to join him for a
sacrificial feast. As an elder,
it was natural for Yishai to be
invited; but when his sons were
inexplicably also invited, they
worried that perhaps the prophet
had come to publicly reveal the
embarrassing and illegitimate
origins of their brother.
Unbeknownst to them, Samuel
would anoint the new king of
Israel at this feast. All that
had been revealed to the prophet
at this point was that the new
king would be a son of Yishai.

When they came, Samuel saw Eliav
(Yishai's oldest son), and he
thought, "Surely God's anointed
stands before Him!"

But God said to Samuel, "Don't
look at his appearance or his
great height, for I have
rejected him. God does not see
with mere eyes, like a man does.
God sees the heart!"

Then Yishai called Avinadav (his
second son), and made him pass
before Samuel. He said: "God did
not choose this one either."

Yishai made Shammah pass, and
Samuel said, "God has not chosen
this one either."

Yishai had his seven sons pass
before Samuel. Samuel said to
Yishai, "God has not chosen any
of them."

*At last Samuel said to Yishai,
"Are there no lads remaining?"*

*He answered, "A small one is
left; he is taking care of the
sheep."*

*So Samuel said to him, "Send for
him and have him brought; we
will not stir until he comes
here."*

*So he sent for him and had him
brought. He was of ruddy
complexion with red hair,
beautiful eyes, and handsome to
look at.*

*God said: "Rise up, anoint him,
for this is the one!"* (<u>I Samuel
16:6-12</u>)

The Small One, Left Behind

As Samuel laid his eyes on
Yishai's eldest son, he was
certain that this was the future

king of Israel. Tall, handsome and distinguished, Eliav was the one whom Samuel was ready to anoint, until God reprimanded Samuel to look not at the outside but at the inside.[8]

No longer did Samuel make any assumptions of his own, but he waited to be told who was to become the next king. All the seven sons of Yishai had passed before Samuel, and none of them had been chosen.

"Are these all the lads?" Samuel asked. Samuel prophetically chose his words carefully. Had he asked if these were all Yishai's *sons*, Yishai would have answered affirmatively, that there were no more of *his sons*, since David was not given the status of a son?

Instead, Yishai answered, "A small one is left; he is taking care of the sheep." David's status was small in Yishai's eyes. He was hoping that Samuel would allow David to remain where he was, out of trouble, tending to the sheep in the faraway pastures.

But Samuel ordered that David immediately be summoned to the feast. A messenger was dispatched to David who, out of respect for the prophet, first went home to wash himself and change his clothes. Unaccustomed to seeing David home at such a time, Nitzevet inquired, "Why did you come home in the middle of the day?"

David explained the reason, and Nitzevet answered, "If so, I too am accompanying you."

As David arrived, Samuel saw a man "of ruddy complexion, with red hair, beautiful eyes, and handsome to look at." David's physical appearance alludes to the differing aspects of his personality. His ruddiness suggests a warlike nature, while his eyes and general appearance indicate kindness and gentility.[9]

At first Samuel doubted whether David could be the one worthy of the kingship, a forerunner of the dynasty that would lead the Jewish people to the end of time. He thought to himself, "This one will shed blood as did the red-headed Esau."[10]

God saw, however, that David's greatness was that he would direct his aggressiveness toward positive aims. God commanded Samuel, "My anointed one is standing before you, and you remain seated? Arise and anoint David without delay! For he is the one I have chosen!"[11]

As Samuel held the horn of oil, it bubbled, as if it could not wait to drop onto David's forehead. When Samuel anointed him, the oil hardened and glistened like pearls and precious stones, and the horn remained full.

As Samuel anointed David, the sound of weeping could be heard from outside the great hall. It was the voice of Nitzevet, David's lone supporter and solitary source of comfort.

Her twenty-eight long years of silence in the face of humiliation were finally coming to a close. At last, all would see that the lineage of her

youngest son was pure, undefiled
by any blemish. Finally, the
anguish and humiliation that she
and her son had borne would come
to an end.

Facing her other sons, Nitzevet
exclaimed, "The stone that was
reviled by the builders[12] has now
become the cornerstone!"
(Psalms118:22)

Humbled, they responded, "This
has come from God; it was hidden
from our eyes" (ibid. verse 23).

Those in the hall cried out in
unison, "Long live the king!
Long live the king!" Within
moments, the once-reviled
shepherd boy became the anointed
future king of Israel.

Nitzevet's Legacy

King David would have many more
trials to face until he was

acknowledged by the entire nation as the new monarch to replace King Saul. During his kingship, and throughout his life, up until his old age, King David faced many ordeals.

King David possessed many great talents and qualities which would assist him in attaining the tremendous achievements of his lifetime. Many of these positive qualities were inherited from his illustrious father, Yishai, after whom he is fondly and respectfully called *ben Yishai,* the son of Yishai.

But it was undoubtedly from his mother that the young David absorbed the fortitude and courage to face his adversaries. From the moment he was born, and during his most tender years, it was Nitzevet who, by example, taught him the essential lesson of valuing every individual's dignity and refraining from embarrassing another, regardless of the personal consequences. It was she who displayed a silent but stoic bravery and dignity in the face of the gravest hardship.

It is from Nitzevet that King David absorbed the strength, born from an inner confidence, to disregard the callous treatment of the world and find solace in the comfort of one's Maker. It was this strength that would fortify King David to defeat his staunchest antagonists and his most treacherous enemies, as he valiantly fought against the mightiest warriors on behalf of his people.

Nitzevet taught her young child to find strength in following the path of one's inner convictions, irrespective of the cruelty that might be hurled at him. Her display of patient confidence in the Creator that justice would be served gave David the inner peace and solace that he would need, over and over again, in confronting the formidable challenges in his life. Rather than succumb to his afflictions, rather than become the individual who was shunned by his tormentors, David learned from his mother to stand proud and dignified, feeling consolation in communicating with his Maker in the open pastures.

She demonstrated to him, as well, the necessity of boldness while pursuing the right path.

When the situation would call
for it, personal risks must be
taken. Without her bold action
in taking the place of her
maidservant that fateful night,
the great soul of her youngest
child, David, the forebear
of Moshiach, would never have
descended to this world.

The soul-
stirring psalms composed by King
David in his greatest hours of
need eloquently describe his
suffering and heartache, as well
as his faith and conviction. The
book of Psalms gives a voice to
each of us, and has become the
balm to soothe all of our
wounds, as we too encounter the
many personal and communal
hardships of life
in *galut* (exile).

As we say these verses, our
voices mesh with Nitzevet's,
with King David's, and with all
the voices of those past and
present who have experienced
unjustified pain, in beseeching
our Maker for that time when the
"son (descendant) of David" will
usher in the era of redemption,
and true justice will suffuse
creation.

FOOTNOTES

1.

Translation taken from *The
Living Nach*, published by
Moznaim.

2.

Siftei Kohen, Vayeishev.

3.

See I Samuel17:34-36

4. The story and concepts in this chapter are based on *Yalkut HaMachiri*, as well as *Sefer HaTodaah* (section on Sivan and Shavuot). See also an interesting English rendition in the book *Don't Give Up*, pp. 187ff.

5.

See Genesis ch. 38, and Midrashim and commentaries on that chapter.

6.

In the verse in the psalm where David says he was a "stranger" to his brothers, the Hebrew word for stranger, *muzar*, is from the same root as *mamzer*—bastard, illegitimate offspring.

7.

Commentaries of Radak and
Abarbanel to 1 Samuel 16:3.

<u>8.</u>

A short while after this
coronation feast, David was
instructed by his father to
visit Eliav at the battlefield.
A war with the Philistines was
imminent, and Eliav lashed out
in anger at David. This tendency
to anger disqualified Eliav now
from the throne. (This event
occurred after David was
anointed as king. However,
according to the commentaries,
it is possible that they didn't
understand the implications of
the anointing, assuming that
Samuel had designated David as a
new student in his school of
prophecy. Though this was an
honor, and an act that would
validate David's lineage, only

once David actually became king over the entire nation did his brothers realize his true greatness.)

9.

Malbim.

10.

Bereishit Rabbah 63:8.

11.

Midrash Tanchuma, Va'eira 6.

12.

The Hebrew word in this verse for "builders," *bonim*, is the same root as the word for "sons.

The keys of David in my hands

In the book of Isaia55:3- 5 we
read:"

Give ear and come to me;
    listen, that you may live.
I will make an everlasting
covenant with you,
    my faithful love promised to
David.
See, I have made him a
witness to the peoples,
    a ruler and commander of the
peoples.
 Surely you will summon
nations you know not,
    and nations you do not know
will come running to you,
because of the Lord your God,
    the Holy One of Israel,
    for he has endowed you with
splendor." New International
Version.

I was then stirred up by the Holy Spirit to receive those promises from God. Jesus said that when we ask we have to believe we have received.

Another word says that the descendants of David will lead like God , like angel of God.

On that day the LORD will shield those who live in Jerusalem, so that the feeblest among them will be like David, and the house of David will be like God, like the angel of the LORD going before them. Zechariah 12:8, New International Version.

Through Christ I am a descendant of David. Therefore this promise is mine. I will rule like God, like Jesus and like an angel of God.

The bible says also that Jesus
has he keys of David.

But What is the key of David and
what does it symbolize?

Well. The key of David appears
only twice in the Bible. The
first time it appears is in
Revelation where it states, "To
the angel of the church in
Philadelphia write . . . who
holds the KEY OF DAVID"
(Revelation 3:7). The speaker is
the resurrected Jesus, whom John
sees in a vision, and the
message is to the church at
Philadelphia. The possession of
this key by Christ is used as
proof that the being addressing
the church is God, "the Holy
One, the One Who is true."

The second occurrence of the key
of David is in the book of
Isaiah the prophet where it

states, "And the key of the
house of David will I lay upon
his shoulder (Eliakim as an
allusion or type of Christ); so
he shall open, and none shall
shut; and he shall shut, and
none shall open" (Isaiah 22:22,
KJV).

In short the key of David in the
hands of Jesus means Power and
authority, the ability to unlock
or lock something.
  Since the descendants of David
will rule like God and we know
that Jesus is God. Therefore I
will rule holding the keys of
David as well.

You can ask before I continue :"
Is Jesus really God?". The
answer is yes like what I said
in the book:" One world , one

nation under one God, Jesus Christ."

Jesus is God of gods and Lord of lords.

One day I was discussing with a friend of mine who was a member of Jehovah witness. He was telling me that Jesus is not God the creator. He used some scriptures and I demonstrated that Jesus is the only true God the creator of the universe as described in the holy bible. When I showed him another scripture that proved him wrong, he said:" I am going to rethink about that."The devil knows that once we acknowledge Jesus as God and not as a mere prophet like Moses and Elijah, then we have won over him.

Jesus is the Jehovah but who came in the world with a human body in the name of Jesus. In the plan of God was to reveal himself to His created and teach them how to worship the true God, their maker. Before Jesus came, God used Moses, prophets as the mediator between a man and God. They were human beings and therefore they were imperfect vessels of God. There was a need of a perfect one who is God himself. And that was His majesty Jesus Christ the living True God.

Water that is pure and passes through an impure pipe becomes contaminated with some impurity. The water is no longer pure and it is not good for health.

Our heavenly father used to send human beings to teach his law

*like Moses and other prophet
like the Prophet Elijah but they
were like imperfect pipe,
imperfect vessels. God had to
come down himself in the name of
Jesus Christ to teach us how to
love him and worship in the
proper manner.*

*Jesus was without sin because He
is God. He was not from Adam.
Jesus asked Pharisees:" Can any
of you prove me guilty of sin?
If I am telling the truth, why
don't you believe me? John 8:46,
New International Version.*

*You cannot remove a sin while
yourself you have sins. So Jesus
because He was God therefore He
was the right one to come in the
world and take away the sin of
the world caused by the
rebellion of Adam.*

He is from heaven, from God himself. In the book of <u>Luke 1:35</u> . We read:"The angel answered and said to her (Mary the mother of Jesus), "The Holy Spirit will come upon you and the power of the Most High will overshadow you; and for that reason the holy Child shall be called the Son of God.

It appears at John 1:29, where John the Baptist sees Jesus and exclaims, "Behold the Lamb of God who takes away the sin of the world."

Jesus knew and defended that He was God. Jesus, in response to the Pharisees' question "Who do you think you are?" said, "'your father Abraham rejoiced at the thought of seeing my day; he saw it and was glad.' 'You are not yet fifty years old,' the Jews said to him, 'and you have seen Abraham!' 'I tell you the truth,' Jesus answered, 'before Abraham was born, I am!' At this, they picked up stones to stone him, but Jesus hid himself, slipping away from the temple grounds" (John 8:56–59). The violent response of the Jews to Jesus' "I AM" statement indicates they clearly understood what He was declaring—that He was the eternal God incarnate. Jesus was equating Himself with the "I AM" title God gave Himself in Exodus 3:14.

If Jesus had merely wanted to say He existed before Abraham's time, He would have said, "Before Abraham, I was." The Greek words translated "was," in the case of Abraham, and "am," in the case of Jesus, are quite different. The words chosen by the Spirit make it clear that Abraham was "brought into being," but Jesus existed eternally (see John 1:1).

There is no doubt that the Jews understood what He was saying because they took up stones to kill Him for making Himself equal with God (John 5:18). Such a statement, if not true, was blasphemy and the punishment prescribed by the Mosaic Law was death (Leviticus 24:11-14). But Jesus committed no blasphemy; He was and is God, the second Person of the Godhead, equal to the Father in every way.

To the all my beloved and great people who are in Judaism and Islam, I would like to show again that the God of Jacob, the

God of Abraham has been revealed to the World in the name of Jesus Christ.

In the book of Revelation 22:13 Jesus said to Apostle John:"I am the Alpha and the Omega, the first and the last, the beginning and the end."; we read also in Revelation 1:8:"I am the Alpha and the Omega," says the Lord God, "who is and who was and who is to come, the Almighty."; Revelation 21:6 :"Then He said to me, "It is done I am the Alpha and the Omega, the beginning and the end I will give to the one who thirsts from the spring of the water of life without cost."

Let me also add the verses respectively Revelation 1:17 and Revelation 2:8 :"When I saw Him, I fell at His feet like

a dead man And He placed His
right hand on me, saying, "Do
not be afraid; I am the first
and the last, "And to the angel
of the church in Smyrna write:
The first and the last, who was
dead, and has come to life, says
this:"

In the old testament we find
that Jesus is the same in old
testament and the new testament
when we read in the book of
Isaiah where the God of Jacob
called himself like the First
and the Last:"

<u>Isaiah 44:6</u>"Thus says the LORD,
the King of Israel and his
Redeemer, the LORD of hosts: 'I
am the first and I am the last,
and there is no God besides Me.

<u>Isaiah 48:12</u>"Listen to Me, O
Jacob, even Israel whom I

called; I am He, I am the first, I am also the last.

<u>*Isaiah 41:4*</u>*"Who has performed and accomplished it, Calling forth the generations from the beginning? 'I, the LORD, am the first, and with the last I am He.'""*

These verses demonstrate that Jesus is the Same God in the Old Testament and in the New Testament.

Jesus is given the name of Lord of lords in the New Testament which is also found in the Old Testament meaning that Jesus Christ is the same God in the Old Testament and in the New Testament:

Proof in the New Testament

In Revelation 19:16 we read:"On his robe and on his thigh he has

*a name written, King of
kings and Lord of lords." And we
read also in Revelation
17:14 They will make war on the
Lamb, and the Lamb will conquer
them, for he is Lord of
lords and King of kings, and
those with him are called and
chosen and faithful."*

*Proof of the calling of God the
Lord of lords from the Old
Testament.*

*Deuteronomy 10:17:" For
the Lord your God is God of gods
and Lord of lords, the great,
the mighty, and the awesome God,
who is not partial and takes no
bribe.";*

*Psalm 136:2-3: "Give thanks to
the God of gods.
His love endures forever.*

*Give thanks to the Lord of
lords,*

*For his steadfast love endures
forever;"*

*This is the proof that our
beloved Lord and Savior Jesus
Christ is the same God in the
Old Testament and the New
Testament. He is the God of
gods; the God of Abraham, Isaac
and Jacob who created us and who
deserves and he
only worship forever and
ever. There is no power, no
king, and no lord who can oppose
Him and win! Hallelujah!
Halleluiah!*

*Shame the devil by your worship
while kneeling down*

*Satan always look the best that
God always look for because he*

knows what that is the best God desires a lot that moves His heart.

When Satan was tempting he told Jesus:" If you bow down and worship me, I will give all the kingdoms of the earth!" But our always overcomer, our good friend Jesus Christ rebuked Satan and said:" It is written you shall worship God and serve Him only!"

This kind of worship is the best that the devil was looking from His Creator Jesus Christ for Satan to grant to Jesus the kingdoms of the world.

asking for Jesus to

I like to worship my Lord Jesus Christ and spend some times before the Lord kneeling down as a sacrifice of thanksgiving for having died for me and the whole world just to shame the devil.

One day I ask a certain pastor:" Here in Zambia you like to kneel down to show a respect to someone who deserve honor but how many times do you kneel down when you are praying God?"

It is no easy to kneel down; it is painful. Then I understood why to kneel down in worship to God is the best because it is a sacrifice in its own.

One night I was praying and took more than one hour praying kneeling down to shame the devil and I heard a voice saying like:" If you worship me and bow down before me, I will make everything bow down to you!" In order words God will make turn a "none" into a "yes". He will

*make disobedient people obedient
by His power.*

*He will make what is impossible
possible. He will make all
rulers of the earth obey and
serve me! God instructed princes
through the prophet of God
Ezechiel to bow down in worship
while in temple! If you do not
have your legs, you can still
worship God in your heart
because the true worshipper God
is looking for is a person who
worships God in true and in
Spirit and that means worship
out of your heart.*

*God is interested by a true
worship from your heart
expressed physically knelling
down or lifting up your hands as
a sign of surrender the own
Moses used to overcome the enemy
while Joshua was on the ground*

fighting against the enemy. Any revelation that worked in the past was also revealed to us in our time. But the Holy Spirit is the one who can lead you what kind of weapon you need to use in prayer for a particular situation.

My beloved people from all the world let's spend some times kneeling down in worship before the King of kings our Lord, and God Jesus Christ and give this kind of worship to Jesus for the glory of our heavenly Father and bring shame to the devil.

Keys of David used for the
victory of Donald Trump in 2016

I am used using the keys of
David to resolve some issues
against the will of God. Before
I speak about my beloved and
great man Donald Trump, a man
who likes to keep his words. I

used the power behind the keys
of David for Ben LADEN BEFORE
Donald Trump.

Do you want to know how?

The end of Osama Ben Laden
How did I use the key of David I
understood that when God has
given you something it is
already there that is why He
said believe that you have
already received whatever you
ask for. That means in Heaven
they know they have already a
King over all the Earth who
comes in the name of Jesus. When
I gave myself to our beloved
Heavenly Father in the name of
Jesus Christ, I said:" Lord here
I am, send me Lord I am ready to
rule the whole world like your
David king in my time"

After that The Holy Spirit led
to a verse I had not yet known
before written in Zechariah14.9:
"The Lord will be king over the
whole earth. On that day there
will be one Lord, and his name
the only name." New
International Version. When I
saw this prophecy I realized I
am under a divine mission to
fulfill this prophecy.

In the time Of David the throne
of David was also a throne of
God; His kingdom was The Lord's.
That is why God said I watch
over your kingdom why? Because
it was His. So the success of
the David in what right in the
eyes of God was God's therefore
it was impossible to fail for
David. The Lord made sure he
succeeded where he went and
became more powerful than his
enemies.

We are in the right time for the Lord to be king over all the earth through me. There is television; the time has come for the ruling of his king David in his name.

Another vow I did to the Lord Jesus Christ is to remove all idols once a King. After that vow, the Holy Spirit led me to a prophecy written in Zechariah 13Zechariah13.2: "On that day, I will banish the names of the idols from the land, and they will be remembered no more," declares the Lord Almighty. "I will remove both the prophets and the spirit of impurity from the land. New International Version. I understood that all those vows are inspired by the Holy Spirit to do his will on the Earth.

I understood I am sent by heaven
to establish His kingdom on
Earth and to do his will on
earth as it is in heaven. In
heaven there is only one God, no
other idols. If God is for me
who can be against me? It is a
divine agenda. God always stir
up a man to fulfill divine
purpose. We are in the time of
God and He will make sure He
succeeds because no man can
obstruct his purpose.

Let me tell you another strange
thing happened in Burundi:

A powerful man of God the late
Dr Myles Munroe came in Burundi
before in his last days of
life. He was preaching in the
Church called Living Church of
Jesus Christ". Suddenly, I heard
a voice in me:" This man is
going to die". I said maybe it

is just a voice! After Burundi
he went in Kenya, and I was told
that in Kenya he said: "My
mission here on earth is over. I
am empty I am ready to go back
home. After those words his
private jet crashed." He died
with his wife. Then I remembered
the voice. I couldn't believe he
really died. I remembered that
what I said if David a prophet
that meant God will use also as
his prophet.

What Dr Myles Munroe used to
preach was to teach people to
establish the Kingdom of God on
Earth. Why God is he foretelling
me his death? Maybe because what
he was preaching to people it
was a burning dream to apply
what he was teaching all over
the world.

Was Dr Myles Munroe my forerunner or was he like John to Jesus?

His key verse was contained in The prayer of our Lord and God Jesus to his disciples, when you pray say:" Our heavenly Father, Hallowed be your name, may your kingdom come! May your will be done on the earth as it is in heaven!

What is the name that Jesus was talking about that must be honored on the earth? Of course the name of Jesus Christ. What? Yeah, when Jesus was praying: he said: Father, I protected those you gave me in your name you gave me. The name of Jesus! Jesus and the Father they are one.

When Apostle Paul was still called Saul persecuting the

followers of Jesus , He caught
him by force and Saul asked? Who
are you Lord? He answered: "I am
Jesus you are persecuting.
Meaning Jesus is ruling like a
lion but not like a lamb. A lion
is in charge of the jungle. It
is not a democracy it is a
kingdom!

In psalm 2:8-9 Jesus asked David
his king: *"If you ask, I will
give you nations, everyone will
be yours. You will rule them
with great power, you will
scatter your enemies like broken
pieces of pottery.''*

I remember one day I said my
dear Lord Jesus Christ, I
believe in every word you have
written or say. That is why I
said that I have asked nations
and they are mine they are my
people and I started loving and

praying for all nations as my
beloved people.

I started stared following what
is happening around our dear
globe. I intercede for the world
as my own people as one people.
When others are busy praying for
their own nation, my concern is
the whole world including. The
world is now like a small
village.

In 2001, right on our
Television, what was happening
was horrible: The 9/11, the
"black" day to USA. The great
nation in the world full of
intelligent people, full of
nuclear weapons and all kind of
arms was beat and hit by mere
human beings. My beloved
American people were injured of
a group of people. The bible
says "_If the LORD does not build

the house; it is useless for the builders to work on it. If the LORD does not protect a city, it is useless for the guard to stay alert." Psalm 127:1 (GW)

It was not an attack only to USA but to the Whole world.

In 2011, I was in my praying room right in Bujumbura, and the Spirit took over me and I said with all my heart: Lord, remember that anyhow America is a nation according the forefathers of USA used Bible for the constitution. Most of missionaries are from USA all over the world like those I worked with in the Burundi at a hospital of kibuye where I operated as a replacer of a medical whom doctor American in the Pediatric service. I was very happy to work with them.

Those guys were good and hardworking. They helped a lot the people of that region Of Burundi in the province of Gitega.

I remember Dr John a tall man, who was operating as ophthalmologist. One day Dr John asked me:"

Where did you get English from? Have you ever travelled? I negatively replied him.

In Burundi we speak French but these days we also speak English because Burundi is also in East Africa community. But I wanted to know English because it is like English is known almost all over the world. So English help to connect with people from all over the world. When I am speaking English I want to speak like American maybe that is why some American friends tell me I speak well English.

So attack America meant to attack me it is like to attack Israel as well. I love America and I love Israel too.

So, in my room I said Lord, if you gave me the key of David: what I open no one can shut what I shut no one can open. This a prayer that I used to confess even when I am with others, and one of my friend told me : It is not what you are asking that everybody can ask there is something what God has put on your heart that will be your own burden but not for everybody. I remember what the Savior of the Whole World said: "You cannot receive this saying unless, to whom it is given. " Matthew 19Matthew19.11.

Then I prayed America is like to attack Christianity, those who attacked America came in the name of a religion; and then I said: Lord Jesus let Ben Laden be captured by America. If America it is Christ who wins, but if not then Islam would think they won. I SHOUTED: "IN THE NAME OF Jesus Christ I arrest Ben Laden!"

Some days I heard that Ben Laden was died. What happened It was only God who used those intelligent soldiers.

Obama was pushed by a hand behind the scene .The Hand of God. There were not sure of victory, Obama was advised by his men not to go for the mission because it was really risky.

I advice all my beloved human
beings liked me who are in Islam
to love Christ Jesus like their
God and Savior. Only him He is
worthy of worship all over the
World!

Trump VICTORY

During 2016 US elections this
great woman Hillary Clinton had
a bigger support than Trump.
Hillary was supported by Obama.
Hillary had a lot of Money in
her campaign more than Trump.
Hillary had the main media
behind her while Trump was not.
He chose to use Facebook and
Tweeter.

I like Obama but I hated what He
did in supporting homosexuality
instead of helping our beloved
people under the bad spirit of
homosexuality to get rid of it
so that instead of adopting

children because they were created to have children of their own through heterosexuality. Homosexuality is a sickness and the world must fix it. When you support a sin you became weak. Hillary was not saying against homosexuality meaning she was going to continue what Obama was doing.

Obama is married to his lovely wife Michelle Obama why not help others who are in the wrong way to become normal like him? I read on internet that if you support homosexuality vote Hillary but if not vote Trump.

I said: "Lord Trump must win in the name of Jesus Christ. If you made the first born of all rulers oh Lord, then I allow Trump to win. I started following polls. When I was praying Trump would go up in the polls but when not praying Hillary, that courageous lady would lead the polls.

That remembered what happened with Moses whenever he would raise his hands in prayer Israel would win but when not the enemy would lead the battle. Moses was on the mountain praying while Joshua was the commander on the ground but all eyes were on Moses. Aaron, the brother to Moses realized that, He put Moses on a stone and help Moses to hold his hands up until the total victory.

When I realised how things were going on. I started praying continually until the day before the general elections. Trump won because God was for him. My beloved people in Democrats were

surprised of the victory. They
think it is the president Putin
of my beloved great people of
Russia who became wiser than
Obama in refusing homosexuality
that Obama was supporting that
enabled Trump to win.

It is Jesus Christ was against
you! Homosexuality is a serious
sin that brings a curse to
people and defile the earth and
whoever is supporting it is an
enemy of the people because he
is helping them to their auto
destruction. You are
annihilating their future
generation in them. Jesus is the
same in the time of Sodom and
Gomorrah, today and forever. I
love Obama. He is courageous
brilliant, intelligent but I did
not like the support for
protecting a sin instead of
fighting to find out a way to

help and save our beloved people under the spirit of homosexuality.

But do you know there is a reward to people who follows and fight for the righteousness of God? Jesus Christ the Savior of the Earth said that "happy are those who are pure in the heart for they shall see God" meaning they shall experience the miraculous salvation from God, they shall see his power in their life.

I am a witness for that how righteousness benefit everyone who practices it! Do you want to know about my experience? :

When I reached Zambia, my visa was about to expire, I rushed to the border to renew my visa. The government had already given me a letter that allow me to serve

my beloved great Zambian people
as their medical doctor but an
immigration officer wanted me to
give them some money. For what?
Corruption?

''If you don't have the money
then I will put in jail!'' The
chief intimidated me. I told him
I do not have the money they
asking me. They were working for
the government of this great
man, a man I love who declared
October 18th of every year a
"national prayer day", the
president Edgar c. Lungu which
government had accepted to give
me a job but these people was
acting against the government.

They wanted me to give them $300
and they pushed me to pay them
quickly otherwise the following
day I would pay $400. You know
what? The $300 was the exact

money for the license from the healthy profession council of Zambia? A friend of mine heard already promised to pay that money for the license. When they heard there is someone who is ready to pay that money, they told me to call him and bring them the money. I called friend and he said that he was going to come the following day. They told me while we are waiting for your friend we are going to put in a hotel.

But, the chief called and told me:" Here there is no comedy, you pay the money or we put in jail!"

"Sir, I told you I do not have money now but if the Lord God to put me in jail pleases do it! "I replied him fixing my eyes to him without fear.

"I am done", the chief commanded a woman immigration officer who tried to look for a way to save me from the chief but in vain. May God bless and guide in the ways of the righteousness all women from all over the World!

They put me in a police cell with other Zambians who were there some because of a crime they committed and other foreigners who were there because they entered Zambia without passport, without visa.

An immigration officer who took me to the cell told me He is going to put in the cell while they are waiting for the money.

"It is a command from the chief otherwise you do not deserve the cell." The immigration officer explained to me.

In the cell everyone liked me and they wondering why they put me there. It was a small room with a lot of people. I felt compassion for those people.

Once in the cell they started getting a lot of food from different people more than what they were getting before me.

"Doctor abwera bwino (meaning This doctor has Come with blessings)!"One of my friends in the cell told his friend using the Zambian local language.

This is the same thing my beloved Aunt and her great husband told me once I was already in Zambia. They told me that I was a source of blessing to them while I was staying with them at their home. I stayed with them for many years up to the day I left Burundi to

Zambia. Her husband, a great man
that I love prayed for me the
night before I left Burundi.
That unforgettable night tears
came out of my eyes. I was going
to miss them!

My dearest own father told me
you are "Nizigiyimana" (meaning
in God I trust) God will be with
you! I am grateful to my dearest
wonderful and Almighty heavenly
Father for choosing my father as
my biological father! He is a
man of faith!

What they said what the Lord
Jesus promised me:

*"All nations shall serve you and
they shall be blessed through
you!*

*They will pray for you and bless
you.*

In your time righteousness and prosperity shall abound!"

I give you my righteousness and my justice. Leaders will bring you gifts will bring you precious gifts…"psalm72:1-end

When I was in the cell people told me that pray God that the your friend come quickly otherwise you will go in the court after some 1or 2 months like us and you are not going to win in the court because you are a foreigner.

Thank you for telling me that. I said whether my friend comes or not I will come out here as a free man.

I prayed:" remember my God that I have been praying for Zambia as my own people starting to the president Lungu;

Remember also I did not commit adultery when that man wanted to pay for me an Indian prostitute woman in Zambia because it was a sin to you (although there is a pleasure but it is not a right pleasure. It is something that takes someone to auto destruction.)

Therefore my God do not allow them to put me in court and let me leave this cell as a free man without any my handcuffs on my hands.

Another thing in the in the cell it was hot. I wanted to bath but there was no water. The only water that was there was for the chief within the cell.

"Unless water is coming out of
the tab inside the cell, all of
these people cannot bath." One
of my friend Burundian but
entered Zambia as a Congolese
who was crossing Zambia toward
South Africa the land of the
late Nelson Mandela, gave me the
condition for me to bath. He was
there for two months.

I prayed: "Lord, I want to bath,
please let the water comes
through the tap so that I can
bath and change the climate;
Remove hotness in the cell all
the time I am in the cell!"

In the evening, it rained (it
was a rainy season but the day I
visited the cell it was not
raining for some days. The sun
was hitting seriously Lusaka the
capital of the great Christian
nation of Zambia) and the water

came out of the tap. All the
prisoners went to bath one by
one! I was happy the answer to
my prayer that was benefiting
other people as well. They were
blessed through me God is
faithful where you are. His
promises are yes and amen
through Christ. I love the way
our beloved Jesus Christ the God
of gods and Lord of lords is
faithful. I love righteousness.

Can I tell you that the hotness
disappeared from that day up to
the day I left the cell on the
fifth day? Our God is awesome!
The night before the fifth day
which was the last day in the
cell, I was reading Psalm71
where David was asking God to
give a command and save him.

"*Be my rock of refuge,*
    to which I can always go;

give the command to save me,
*   for you are my rock and my*
fortress." Psalm71:3. New
International Version.

Then I heard the Holy Spirit telling me:"give a command yourself to come out of the cell!" I ten commanded in the name of Jesus as I was told.

You can't believe that early in the morning of the fifth day of my visitation in that dark "world", I heard people calling me:'' Burundian wake up you are called by an immigration officer!" I was released without going in the court what amazed a policeman who asked me:"How come you are released without going in the court?"; others left the place with handcuffs but me nothing was on my hands I left the cell as a free man back to town with a new visa without paying any money according to my prayer to my beloved God in whom I trust. People in the cell, Zambians were happy I was released. They loved me.

They were truly my friends! I advised them during the last night to behave well honoring God in the society once they are released. Like Joseph in prison I was respected in the cell. In the same night I talked to them that some of them were going to be released miraculously the following day.

The day I was made free there 2 young men who were released miraculously and they praised God and told me:" God is big!", "yes He is". I agreed with them! Maybe I was sent in the cell for them and for the release of all

so called foreigners that I
found there because none of them
remained there! I like to see
people are happy; I love the
people, the sheep of God! Jesus
said to Peter if you love me
take care of my sheep!

I praise my heavenly father for
have put climate in my hands in
the name of Jesus. The key of
David was working perfectly: "to
open and no one can shut, to
shut and no one can open."I
praise also my savior and my
rock Jesus Christ for
remembering my righteousness and
saved from the hands of that
immigration officer in charge
who escorted when I was
released. Was he apologizing? I
don't know but we separate
peacefully and I told him:
"Thank you and God bless you!"

What is making Trump strong

When I see what Donald Trump is
doing I do not doubt His success
even against impeachment. He is
a human being but his strength
is that he tries to stand for
what God loves. When you stand
for Jesus God stands for you.
That makes your enemies hard to
overcome you if they are not
hurt.

First all I would start by his
desire to see the American
people more prosperous in
creating more jobs. What you
have is what you give. As a
father fight for His children

that is how Trump is making sure
that all Americans are well
treated. He is making sure that
his people are well fed in
bringing more companies home.

When Jesus was on earth, He
would feed His people. Therefore
when your dream is to create
jobs , bringing opportunities to
people; it means you are trying
to make sure your people are fed
by giving what they can give
them enough money for them using
their hands and skills.

That mindset makes you stronger
because you are fighting for the
interest of people as a good
father. The love always makes
people stronger because God
always support caregivers
thinking good for His people
that Jesus died for.

I was happy als when I read what
my beloved and great Donald
Trump is doing for Christ.

President Trump is Committed to
Protecting Religious Freedom in
the United States and Around the
World

Quote:

Each of us has the right to
follow the dictates of our
conscience and the demands of
our religious conviction.

President Donald J. Trump

ADVANCING RELIGIOUS FREEDOM
AROUND THE WORLD: President
Donald J. Trump is putting
religious freedom on center
stage at the United Nations.

President Trump is hosting the
Global Call to Protect Religious
Freedom event, calling on the

international community and
business leaders to work to
protect religious freedom.

The President is calling on all
nations to act to bring an end
to religious persecution and
stop crimes against people of
faith.

The State Department has hosted
two Religious Freedom
Ministerials, during which more
than 100 governments and
religious leaders committed to
fight religious persecution.

The Administration is
spearheading the International
Religious Freedom Alliance, an
alliance of nations dedicated to
confronting religious
persecution around the world.

The Administration has taken
steps to protect victims of all
faiths from religious violence.

The Administration will dedicate
an additional $25 million to
protect religious freedom and
religious sites and relics.

The Department of Justice hosted
its Summit on Combating Anti-
Semitism in July.

The United States has provided
humanitarian aid to help
Christians and Yazidis who
suffered at the hands of ISIS
and to help Rohingya Muslim
refugees fleeing persecution.

SAFEGUARDING RELIGIOUS FREEDOM
AT HOME: President Trump has
made it a priority to support
every American's fundamental
right to religious freedom
enshrined in the Bill of Rights.

In 2017, President Trump signed an executive order to advance religious freedom, restoring the ideals that have undergirded our Nation since its founding.

The President took action to ensure Americans and organizations are not forced to violate their religious or moral beliefs by complying with Obamacare's contraceptive mandate.

The Department of Health and Human Services (HHS) established a new Conscience and Religious Freedom division to help direct the agency's efforts to protect religious freedom.

HHS took action to protect the right of healthcare entities to act according to their conscience.

This year, the Administration finalized a rule providing more flexibility for Federal employees whose religious beliefs require them to abstain from work on certain days.

The Administration has unequivocally stood for religious freedom in the courts.

COMBATING A GLOBAL CRISIS: The Trump Administration's efforts to advance religious freedom are vital to combating rising levels of violence around the globe.

Eighty-three percent of the world's population lives in nations where religious freedom is threatened or banned.

The Trump Administration is deeply concerned for the more than 1 million Uighurs interned in Chinese internment camps.

Christians are the most persecuted religious group in the world.

Jews, Christians, Muslims, Buddhists, Hindus, Sikhs, Baha'is, humanists, and non-believers alike—almost every group has been increasingly persecuted over the past decade."

https://www.whitehouse.gov/briefings-statements/president-trump-committed-protecting-religious-freedom-united-states-around-world/.

Another thing Trump is doing is to fight for the voiceless people like the unborn people. According to Reuters (Published: 5:48am, 19 Jan, 2019) "US President Donald Trump spoke in a pre-recorded video to thousands of anti-abortion

activists in Washington on
Friday for the 46th March for
Life, vowing to veto any
legislation that "weakens the
protection of human life". That
is a courageous for the
voiceless people in the womb of
their mothers who are supposed
to protect with all their
strength before even an outsider
intervene like President Trump.
That makes Donald Trump
stronger.

Remember what Jesus said:"He who
has found his life will lose it,
and he who has lost his life for
My sake will find it." Matthew
10:39, New American Standard
Bible.

That means to fight for a life
of innocent people like unborn
babies, those weak people. God
is for them and whenever you

fight for them you are fighting for God and Jesus said: "And the King will say, 'I tell you the truth, when you did it to one of the least of these my brothers and sisters, you were doing it to me!' Matthew 25:40, New Living Translation.

When Donald Trump is fighting for those precious sisters and brothers that are still in the womb, it means that he is fighting for the King of life Jesus Christ the creator of the mankind.

Jesus told Saul that the people he was persecuting represented Himself. Apostle Paul after being changed from Saul into Paul reported what happened that day with Jesus in Acts 26:14:"We all fell to the ground, and I heard a voice say to me in

Aramaic, 'Saul, Saul, why do you persecute Me? It is hard for you to kick against the goads.'"

Trump is fighting against persecution against Christians. He is fighting a divine war. That makes Donald Trump backed by heaven. "If God is for you who can be against us? It is written in Romans 8:31.

Donald Trump is fighting the Lord's battles AND God because of His faithfulness will fight for Him. There is a promise of God in Isaiah41:11-12 for people who is standing for what is right. _"All who rage against you
     will surely be ashamed and disgraced;
those who oppose you
     will be as nothing and

perish.
12 Though you search for your
enemies,
     you will not find them.
Those who wage war against you
     will be as nothing at all.
13 For I am the LORD your God
     who takes hold of your right
hand
and says to you, Do not fear;
     I will help you."

That is why I want to tell all
my beloved democrat people and
all my beloved and great people
of America to honor and respect
Donald Trump because if God is
with him you will never win.
Remember when America was
fighting against ISIS, our
beloved and great people were
happy because they saw
themselves backed by America, a
nation that God made powerful
for a reason.

But when Donald Trump removed
the brave US American soldiers
from Syria because he wanted to
keep his promise at all cost of
removing, our beloved Kurds
people found themselves
helpless. They were powerful
when America was there. Imagine
how powerful you are when God is
with you.

If he was trying to investigate
what caused the Ukrainian
prosecutor to be removed from
his position because he was
fighting corruption, I think it
is a wise thing because he is
trying to stand for justice. I
think we should support that. If
there is nothing against my
beloved and great man Joe Biden
then it is okay and that will
make him stronger. I think we
should cerebrate what Trump is
doing. Otherwise it is like you

are protecting our beloved man Joe Biden from a particular crime.

Stand with Donald Trump while He is looking for a way to make America and keep America great.

I would like to end this small book by telling you the vision I had when I was praying in my room concerning the new world order as a holy world holy nation for Christ where New York is like the new Jerusalem as capital city of the new world order under one God Jesus Christ.

God bless America and all the nations including Kurds our beloved people that must preserved as a part of our body.

May Peace, prosperity, righteousness and justice of our

Lord God in the name of Jesus be
the portion for the entire
world. I love you and I pray for
you!

www.ingramcontent.com/pod-product-compliance
Lightning Source LLC
Chambersburg PA
CBHW031248250726
48655CB00005B/2123